DISCOVER AND DO!

ROMANS

GET HANDS-ON WITH HISTORY

Written by Jane Lacey

W

FRANKLIN WATTS

LONDON • SYDNEY

Franklin Watts
First published in Great Britain in 2021
by The Watts Publishing Group
Copyright © The Watts Publishing Group, 2021

 Produced for Franklin Watts by
White-Thomson Publishing Ltd
www.wtpub.co.uk

HB ISBN: 978 1 4451 7729 8
PB ISBN: 978 1 4451 7745 8

Editor: Katie Dicker
Designer: Clare Nicholas
Series designer: Rocket Design (East Anglia) Ltd

Picture credits:
t=top b=bottom m=middle l=left r=right

Shutterstock: Bahau *cover/title page l* and 10b, Kundra *cover/title page r*, Nikola Knezevic 4 and 20b, Macrovector 5tl, 6b,12b and 29b, StockSmartStart 5tr and 25t, GoodStudio 5br, 22b, 26b and 31b, JeniFoto 7t and 32, Peter Hermes Furian 7b, Gilmanshin 8t and 23t, Sentavio 8b, Yaroslaff 9t, Siberian Art 10t and 30b, D.R.3D 11t, BlueRingMedia 13t, Prostock-studio 13b, JethroT 14t, Piranhi 15t, karnavalfoto 16t, steve estvanik 16b, Giamka 18t, A-R-T 18bl, BlackMac 18b, YUCALORA 20t, 29t and 30t, emperorcosar 24t, Malchev 26t and 31m, delcarmat 27t, 28 and 31t; iStock: Bakhauaddin-bek Sopybekov 4 and 20b, wjarek 6t, ZU_09 12t, Khosrork 17b, Keith Lance 21t, clu 24b; Alamy: Album 17t, © Museum of London/Heritage-Images 22t; Getty: Luigi Galante 14b.

All design elements from Shutterstock.
Craft models from a previous series made
by Anna-Marie D'Cruz/photos by Steve Shott.

Every attempt has been made to clear copyright.
Should there be any inadvertent omission, please
apply to the publisher for rectification.

Printed in China

Franklin Watts
An imprint of
Hachette Children's Group
Part of The Watts Publishing Group
Carmelite House
50 Victoria Embankment
London EC4Y 0DZ

An Hachette UK Company
www.hachettechildrens.co.uk

DISCOVER AND DO!

ROMANS

GET HANDS-ON WITH HISTORY

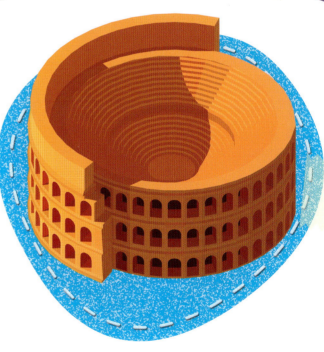

W

FRANKLIN WATTS

LONDON • SYDNEY

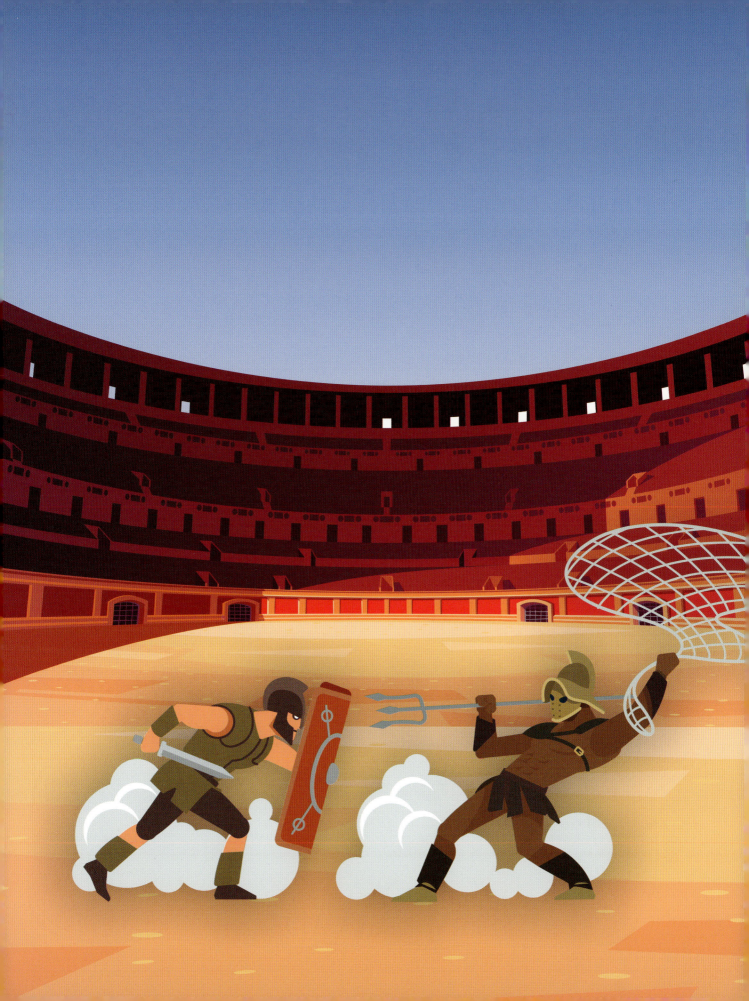

CONTENTS

Words that appear in **bold** can be found in the glossary on pages 28–29.

THE ROMANS

The Romans were the people of the city of Rome. They built a powerful **empire** that lasted for around 500 years from 27 BCE to 476 CE. According to **legend**, Rome was built in 753 BCE by twin brothers Romulus and Remus who were brought up by a mother wolf.

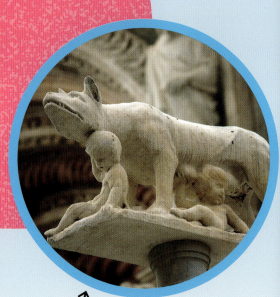

Ancient Rome

The city of Rome became very powerful with grand government buildings, temples, bath houses, theatres and statues. Today, Rome is the capital city of Italy. The remains of ancient Roman buildings can still be seen there.

Rome was named after Romulus. Legend says the twin boys were raised by a wolf.

Roads, bridges and ships

The Romans were clever **engineers**. They built thousands of kilometres of roads with bridges over rivers and valleys, and ships that sailed the Mediterranean Sea. Roads and ships allowed the Romans to travel quickly and **conquer** surrounding countries.

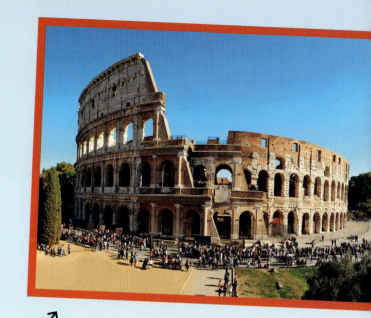

The Colosseum, where Romans watched **gladiators** fight, still stands in Rome today.

Huge empire

With the help of a powerful army, the Roman Empire grew rapidly. At the height of its power, it spread across North Africa right through Europe to far away Britain.

The areas in red show the countries in the Roman Empire.

Britain

Gaul

Spain

Rome

Africa

Syria

Egypt

ROMAN EMPERORS

At first, Rome was ruled by kings and then by an elected **senate**. However, as the city's power grew, **senators** and army generals fought to control Roman lands. Eventually one person took over, the emperor.

A statue of Augustus Caesar, the first emperor.

The first emperor

Many people thought the famous Roman general, Julius Caesar, would be the first Roman emperor. But he was murdered. A few years later, in 27 BCE, his nephew, Augustus Caesar, became the first of 49 emperors.

The senators wore **togas** and leather sandals.

The emperor wore more colourful robes.

Emperor god

Roman emperors were very powerful. The emperor's head was stamped on Roman coins. Emperors were worshipped like gods. Temples were built to them all over the Empire.

These Roman coins show the head of Emperor Trajan who ruled from 98 CE.

ACTIVITY

MAKE A LAUREL WREATH

Emperors were not kings and they did not wear crowns. They wore wreaths made from laurel to celebrate victory and power.

You will need:
- **dark green card**
- **scissors**
- **pencil**
- **glue or sticky tape**

1 Cut out a band of dark green card, about 4 cm wide, to fit around your head.

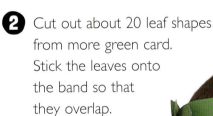

2 Cut out about 20 leaf shapes from more green card. Stick the leaves onto the band so that they overlap.

3 Glue the ends of the band together. Put on your wreath and become a Roman emperor.

THE ARMY

The Roman Empire needed a large army to conquer and control the lands they invaded. The army was important to the emperor and he made sure his soldiers were looked after.

A soldier's life

A soldier joined the army for 25 years. He was paid in money and in salt. During a war, soldiers marched up to 32 kilometres a day, wearing leather sandals and carrying heavy equipment. They built roads and bridges as they went, setting up camp each night.

Soldiers used a stabbing sword and a spear and had metal armour to protect them.

The Roman army was highly trained, but only men were allowed to be soldiers.

Legion

A **legion** was made up of about 5,000 soldiers called legionaries. They were organised into smaller groups of about 100 soldiers called **centuries**, led by an officer called a centurion. Each legion carried an eagle **standard**, which was the symbol of its power.

If a standard was captured by the enemy, the legion broke up.

ACTIVITY

MAKE AN EAGLE STANDARD

You will need:
- card
- pencil
- scissors
- 2 wrapping paper tubes
- silver paint
- 2 red ribbons
- glue or sticky tape

1 Copy the shapes below onto card. You will need three of the circle shape. Make the eagle as big as this page.

2 Using two tubes from rolls of wrapping paper, squash the end of one inside the other.

3 Paint the shapes and tubes with silver paint.

4 Stick the painted shapes onto the pole with the eagle at the top.

5 Decorate with red ribbons to complete the standard.

LIFE IN ROMAN TIMES

Everyone had their place in Roman times. **Citizens** were men who had been born in Rome or had served Rome in a war. Non-citizens were born outside Rome. **Slaves** had no rights and belonged to their owner.

Roman families

The father was the head of a Roman family. He was expected to look after his wife and children, and their slaves. Girls were expected to grow up to be wives and mothers. The women managed the household and the family money. Families sometimes took in and looked after someone who had no family.

This Roman carving shows mother, father and son. The boy is dressed like his father.

Slaves were not paid for their hard work.

Life as a slave

Slaves were either born as slaves or were captives of war. They worked hard as household slaves or on farms or building sites. Slaves were often badly treated, but some owners tried to make them feel part of the family.

Jobs to do

Fetching water

Cleaning

Shopping

Tending the fire

Cooking

Serving at table

Helping the women to dress and do their hair

Looking after the children

ACTIVITY

DAY AS A SLAVE

You will need:

- **paper**
- **pencil and pens**

1 Imagine you are a slave boy or girl in Roman times. Who owns you? How do they treat you?

2 Write about a day in the life of a slave boy or girl.

3 Draw a picture of yourself at work.

Today, important guests are coming to dinner.

I'll be in trouble if anything goes wrong!

HOUSES

A Roman country house was called a **villa**. A town house was called a **domus**. A family would live in one part of a house, with their slaves in the other.

Villas

Remains of Roman villas have been found all over the Roman Empire. They belonged to rich farmers and landowners. They had many rooms, which were richly decorated with wall paintings and statues. Roman houses often had a shady courtyard with a pool to collect rainwater.

In crowded towns, people lived in four- or five-storey apartment blocks called **insulae**, as shown by this ruin.

Can you identify the different rooms of this Roman villa?

Mosaics

Some villas had mosaics. These were pictures and patterns made of small pieces of stone or tiles. The pictures often told stories of gods and goddesses.

This mosaic of Venus, the goddess of love, was found in a Roman villa in the UK.

ACTIVITY

MAKE A ROMAN MOSAIC

You will need:

- **pencil**
- **coloured paper**
- **scissors**
- **glue**

2 Cut out squares from different coloured pieces of paper.

3 Paint one section of your picture at a time with glue.

4 Fill each section with coloured squares.

1 Copy this outline of a Roman mosaic.

CHILDHOOD

The children of slaves and poor people did not go
to school. They had to work as soon as they were big enough.
In richer families, boys went to school or were taught at home.
Girls were sometimes taught to read and write.

Child's play

Some Roman children had dolls and toy animals to play with;
they flew kites and played on swings and see-saws. Children
played board games or other simple games, such as marbles.

Knucklebones was a game
like modern jacks.

This mosaic shows
young children herding
geese as part of
their work.

Growing up

When a new baby was born, it was put at its father's feet. If he accepted the baby, it became part of the family. Children learned to be like their parents. Often, children were given a charm called a bulla to protect them. Boys became adults at 14 and girls when they married at 13 or 14.

Children kept their bulla in a bag, which they wore as a bracelet or necklace.

MAKE A BULLA

You will need:
- air-drying clay
- small square of cloth
- coloured string

1 Think of something that is special to you. It must be something you can model out of clay to be your secret charm.

2 Form a clay model of the item and leave it to dry.

3 Put your charm in a small square of cloth.

4 Tie the ends of the square with coloured string and hang it around your wrist.

LETTERS AND NUMBERS

Latin was spoken in Ancient Rome.
We call Latin a dead language because, today,
no groups speak it in daily conversation.
Many modern languages, including English,
are written in the same alphabet
the Romans used.

Scrolls

The Romans wrote on rolls of **papyrus** called scrolls with pen
and ink. Children practised writing on wax tablets. They scored
letters and numbers with a pointed stylus. The wax could be
scraped off to use again.

This replica of a
wax tablet shows
how it was used.

Roman **numerals** were seven letters.
The year 1576 would be written MDLXXVI.

Choose the font
TIMES NEW ROMAN
on a computer and type
some words in capital
letters. Compare them
to this Roman inscription.

I	1
V	5
X	10
L	50
C	100
D	500
M	1000

NI MINER

AGNAE · L

LIAM · TH

ITOLIVM

RIVOS · VIAM · FLAMINI

M · ATQVE · ATHLETAS · E

MAKE A WAX TABLET

You will need:
- candle
- black and brown card
- scissors
- glue
- pencil

1 Rub the end of a candle all over a piece of black card to make a layer of wax.

2 Cut out a frame of brown card and stick it onto the black card.

3 Use a pencil to score Roman letters and numerals into the wax.

4 When the wax is covered in writing, smooth it with a piece of card.

5 Rub on a new layer of wax and use the tablet again.

ENTERTAINMENT

The Romans celebrated many religious festivals with entertainments. There were three main kinds of entertainment: plays, games and races. These were each held in a specially designed building.

Theatre

Roman theatres could hold thousands of people. Actors were popular stars, just like they are today. The plays were comedies, to make people laugh, or serious tragedies.

Actors wore masks so their expressions could be seen from the back seats.

Games

Roman games were bloody and deadly. They were held in huge **amphitheatres**, like the Colosseum (see page 7), where crowds gathered to watch gladiator fights and re-enactments of wars.

Gladiators were criminals, war captives or slaves. Some were professional fighters.

Chariot races

Chariot races were held in an arena called the circus (or **hippodrome**). Chariots pulled by two or four horses raced around a track. Teams of racers had their own supporters, like football teams have today.

Some chariot races had around 250,000 supporters cheering-on their team.

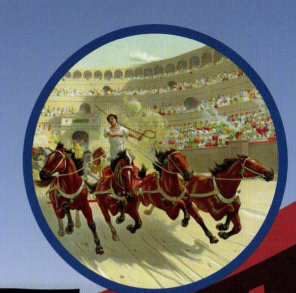

ACTIVITY

MAKE A MODEL CHARIOT

You will need:
- **gold card**
- **pencil**
- **scissors**
- **modelling tool**
- **glue**

1 Copy the shapes below onto gold card and cut out. Score a pattern onto the side with a modelling tool.

2 Snip around the edge of the base and fold up the flaps. Bend the side around the base and glue it onto the flaps.

3 Cut out two card circles 8 cm wide for the wheels and a T-shape for the chariot pole.

4 Either cut out spokes and hub shapes or draw them on. Stick a wheel on each side of the chariot and the T-shape onto the bottom.

← 8 cm →

Flaps

Base

← 10 cm →

← 15 cm →

Side

← 15 cm →

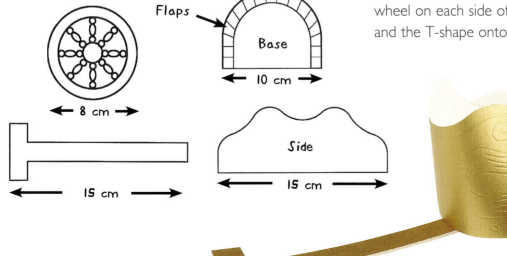

ROMAN BATHS

Public baths were places where people met and relaxed. They had central heating and five different kinds of pools. It only cost a penny to get in.

Hot and cold

The Laconium was a hot room like a sauna with a tub of boiling water. The Caldarium was a hot room with a hot pool. The Tepidarium was a warm room with a warm pool. The Frigidarium had a large, cold pool. The Spa had mineral water to bathe in and drink for good health.

Instead of soap, oil was rubbed onto the skin and scraped off with a metal or bone 'strigil'.

The water in the baths was heated, thanks to fires that warmed the air beneath the floor.

Beauty treatments

Massage, hairdressing, shaving and other beauty treatments were offered at the baths. Slaves helped their masters and mistresses to dress and undress. The clothes were wrapped and held together with belts and pins.

This statue shows how brooches were used to hold folds of fabric together.

ACTIVITY

MAKE A DOLPHIN BROOCH

Ask an adult to help you with this activity

Dolphin shapes were often used in Roman jewellery.

You will need:
- **thick card**
- **coloured shiny card**
- **scissors**
- **glue**
- **silver pen**
- **safety pin**
- **sticky tape**

1 Cut out the shape of a dolphin in thick card.

2 Decorate with shapes of coloured shiny card. Outline the shapes with a silver pen.

3 Tape a safety pin on the back and ask an adult to help you pin it onto your clothes.

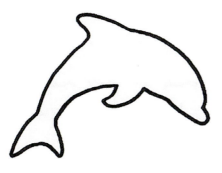

ROMAN TOWNS

In 79 CE, the volcano Vesuvius in Italy erupted and buried the nearby town of Pompeii in ash. The city remained captured in a moment in time under the ash for 1,600 years until it was rediscovered. The remains show us what a Roman town was like.

Layout

Roman towns were surrounded by walls. They often had temples, bath houses, theatres and an amphitheatre. A typical town had two main roads running from north to south and from east to west, meeting at a square in the town centre. Straight streets were lined with gutters that ran into underground sewers.

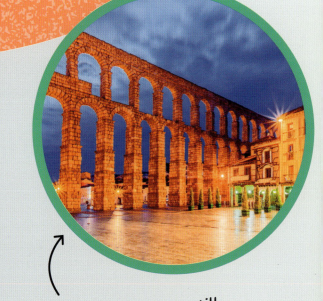

Roman **aqueducts** can still be seen today. They carried fresh water into a town.

The ruins of Pompeii give us important clues about life in a Roman town.

Market goods

The **forum** was a busy market surrounded by shops, snack bars and inns. In the market, you could buy large pottery jars called amphorae, which were used for storing food, and also bowls and plates.

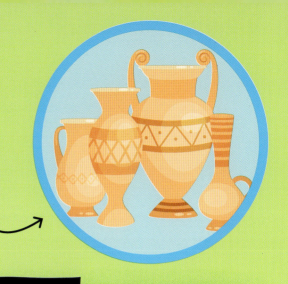

Pottery was made in factories and used all over the Empire.

ACTIVITY

MAKE A SIMPLE COIL POT

You will need:
- **air-drying clay**
- **water**
- **modelling tool**

1 Roll out lots of long sausages of modelling clay.

2 Coil one sausage around to make a flat circle for the base. Damp around the edge with water.

3 Build up the pot with coils of clay, damping with water as you go to stick the layers of clay together.

4 Smooth the sides with a modelling tool and mark on a pattern. Leave to dry.

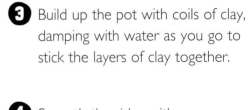

GODS AND MYTHS

The Romans worshipped many gods and goddesses. They believed the gods protected the Roman Empire. Towards the end of the Roman Empire, Christianity became the official religion.

Sacrifice

People brought animals to the temples as a **sacrifice** to please the gods. Priests killed the animals on an **altar** and special requests to the gods were made.

Apollo was the god of sun, light, knowledge, music and poetry.

Jupiter, king of the gods, was the god of thunder and lightning. He carried a lightning bolt.

Ceres, goddess of the harvest, carried ears of corn.

Mars, the god of war, was said to be the father of Romulus and Remus.

Diana, goddess of the moon and hunting, carried a bow and arrow.

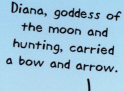

Roman myths

The gods belonged to a family. Stories about them, called myths, explained what happened in the world. Neptune was the god of the sea and earthquakes. He rode a horse in the waves.

Neptune carried a large three-pronged spear called a trident.

ACTIVITY

MAKE A COLLAGE OF A GOD OR GODDESS

Choose a Roman god or goddess. Imagine what they would look like. This is Neptune.

You will need:
- **paper and pencil**
- **scrap material, coloured paper and wool**
- **scissors**
- **glue**

1 Draw your god or goddess carrying their symbol.

2 Use pieces of material, coloured paper and wool to give them clothes and hairstyles in the Roman style.

Glossary

altar

An altar is a table on which sacrifices to the gods were made.

amphitheatre

An amphitheatre is a round- or oval-shaped building where Roman crowds watched gladiator fights.

aqueduct

An aqueduct is a bridge that carries water.

century

In Roman times, a century was a military group of about 100 soldiers, called centuries.

citizen

Roman citizens were men who were born in Rome, or who had fought for Rome. People in conquered lands could also become citizens.

conquer

To attack a place and take control over it. Romans conquered many countries, which then became part of the Roman Empire.

domus

Some wealthy Roman families had a town house called a domus.

empire

An empire is a group of countries ruled by an emperor or empress.

engineer

An engineer is a person who designs and builds roads and bridges.

forum

In Roman times, a public square or marketplace was called a forum.

gladiator

A gladiator was a fighter who entertained Roman crowds.

hippodrome

A hippodrome is an arena. It can have an oval-shaped track for racing.

insulae

Less wealthy Roman families often lived in apartment blocks called insulae.

knucklebones

Knucklebones was a game like modern jacks played with the small bones of animals.

legend

A legend is a traditional story that has been passed down through the ages.

legion

A legion is a large group of soldiers. In the Roman army, a legion had about 5,000 soldiers, called legionaries.

numeral

A numeral is a symbol that stands for a number.

papyrus

Papyrus is a type of paper made from reeds.

sacrifice

A sacrifice is an offering to the gods. Romans brought gifts of food or animals to the temple to be killed to please the gods.

senate

In Roman times, the senate was a group of people who formed part of the government.

senator

A senator was a member of the government who had been voted in by the people.

slave

Slaves are humans owned and forced to work by masters. They are not paid for their work.

standard

A standard was a pole carried by a soldier that had the symbol of his legion on it.

strigil

A strigil was an instrument used by the Romans for scraping the skin after a bath.

toga

A toga was a loose piece of clothing worn in Ancient Rome.

villa

Some wealthy Roman families had a country house called a villa.

Quiz

1 Who was the city of Rome named after?

a) Romeo
b) Romola
c) Romulus
d) Remus

2 Who was the first Roman emperor?

a) Julius Caesar
b) Augustus Caesar
c) Claudius Caesar
d) Nero Caesar

3 On average, how old was a Roman girl when she got married?

a) 10 or 11
b) 13 or 14
c) 16 or 17
d) 18 or 19

4 How long did a soldier serve in the Roman army?

a) 5 years
b) 10 years
c) 20 years
d) 25 years

5 Why did Roman actors wear masks?

a) to hide their faces
b) so everyone could see their expressions
c) so men could act as women
d) so women could act as men

6 How many different letters are used for Roman numerals?

a) five
b) six
c) seven
d) eight

7 Which of the following is NOT a type of Roman bath?

a) Laconium
b) Caldarium
c) Tepidarium
d) Refridgarium

8 Which volcano covered Pompeii in ash?

a) Vesuvius
b) Etna
c) Krakatoa
d) Vulcano

9 **Who was the Roman god of the sun?**

a) Jupiter
b) Ceres
c) Apollo
d) Cupid

10 **What was the name of Neptune's spear?**

a) fork
b) trident
c) bayonet
d) harpoon

ANSWERS 1c, 2b, 3b, 4d, 5b, 6c, 7d, 8a, 9c, 10b

FURTHER INFORMATION

BOOKS

Explore! Romans by Jane Bingham, Wayland

The Genius of: The Romans by Izzi Howell, Franklin Watts

Roman Life: Homes by Nicola Barber and Paul Harrison, Wayland

Invaders and Raiders: The Romans Are Coming! by Paul Mason, Franklin Watts

WEBSITES

Discover 10 fun facts about the Romans www.natgeokids.com/uk/discover/history/romans/10-facts-about-the-ancient-romans

Learn more about life in Roman times www.bbc.co.uk/bitesize/topics/zwmpfg8/articles/z2sm6sg

Find out more about Roman gods and goddesses www.dkfindout.com/uk/history/ancient-rome/roman-gods-and-goddesses

Watch a video about life in Roman Britain www.bbc.co.uk/teach/class-clips-video/history-ks2-life-in-roman-britain-animation/zvdc8xs

Index

Titles in the DISCOVER AND DO! HISTORY series

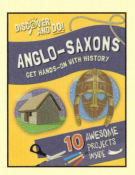

- Invasion
- Warriors
- Settlers
- Village life
- Clothes
- Storytellers
- Death and burial
- Kings and kingdoms
- Gods and goddesses
- Religion
- Runes and writing

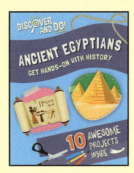

- The Egyptians
- The River Nile
- Egyptian life
- Clothes
- Hair and make-up
- Writing
- Gods and goddesses
- The Pharaoh
- Temple life
- The pyramids
- The afterlife

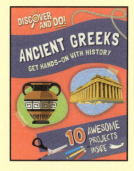

- The Greeks
- City states
- Daily life
- Childhood
- Clothes
- Religion and myths
- Olympic games
- Writing
- Theatre
- Learning
- Famous Greeks

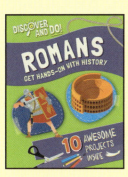

- The Romans
- Roman emperors
- The army
- Life in Roman times
- Houses
- Childhood
- Letters and numbers
- Entertainment
- Roman baths
- Roman towns
- Gods and myths

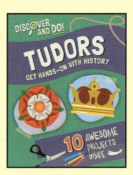

- The Tudors
- Henry VIII
- Life at court
- Tudor homes
- Tudor London
- Street life
- Elizabeth I
- Exploration
- Tudor childhood
- Food
- Theatre

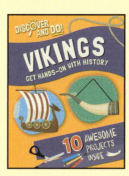

- The Vikings
- Sea journeys
- Warriors
- Viking raids
- Viking houses
- Daily life
- Viking crafts
- Pastimes
- Life and death
- Gods and legends
- Famous Vikings

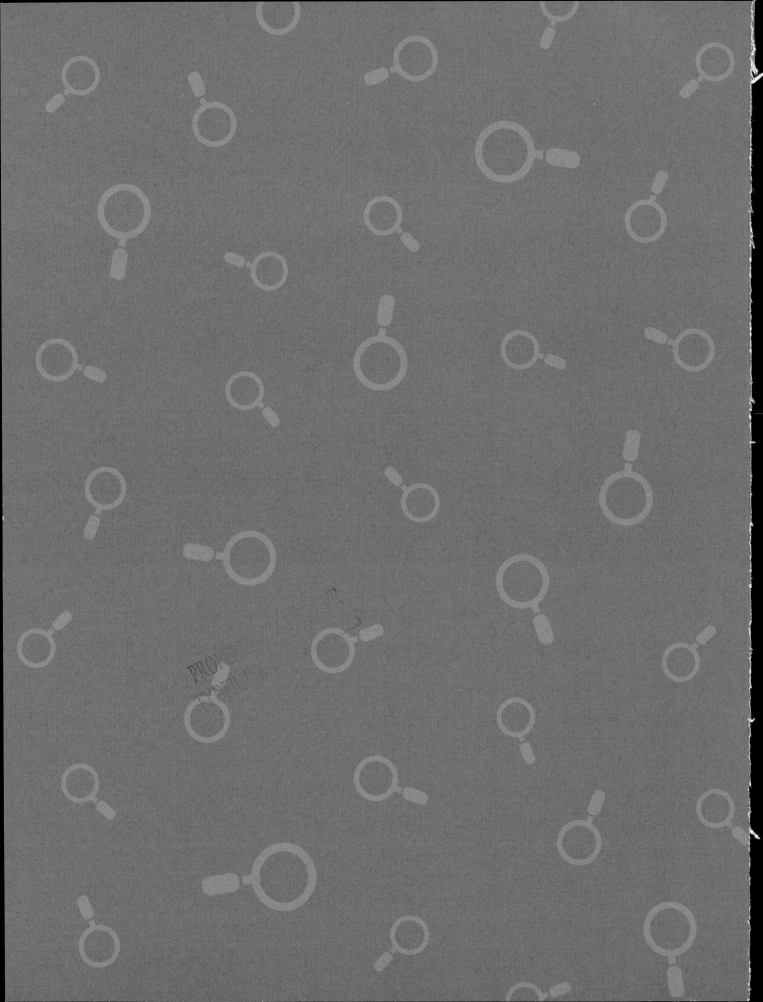